My Voice

Essays on the Warm and Funny Moments of Life

Donna Reed

Published by The News-Gazette

NG

The News-Gazette®

PUBLISHER	John Reed
EDITOR	Jim Rossow
MANAGING EDITOR - ADMINISTRATION	Dan Corkery
MANAGING EDITOR - NEWS	Jeff D'Alessio

Cover design and book layout: Joan Millis, The News-Gazette
Illustrations: Theresa Meacham
  http://theresammeacham.com
  https://www.facebook.com/TMMeacham

ISBN: 978-0-692-46302-4

Printed in the United States of America

The News-Gazette, Inc.
15 Main Street
Champaign, IL 61820
Phone: (217) 351-5252
Fax: (217) 351-5245
www.news-gazette.com

Dedicated to my wonderful family.

Contents

Introduction

Family. Friends. Loved ones. Memories. Moments. *My Voice* is a collection of essays that focus on my life as a wife and mom, teacher, daughter, granddaughter, sister, cousin, aunt, friend and colleague. These essays, first published in *The News-Gazette* in Champaign, Illinois, are comprised of childhood memories, as well as everyday humorous moments and holiday traditions as seen through my eyes and spoken in my voice.

Herein are stories about my brother Mickey's paper route, my mom's wedding gown, my dad's whistle and his "Mick's Sticks," my sister's pilgrim outfit and our annual childhood Christmas play. Also included here are my husband Mike's and my funny holiday stories, our day-to-day snafus and the lessons that our dog, Dudley, always seems to be teaching us. One of life's most rewarding roles for me has been as mother to our wonderful son, Matt. I've become not only the teacher but also the student in this once-in-a-lifetime relationship. Parenting is both exhilarating and humbling, and hopefully I've touched on such emotions in these pages and added a laugh or two as well.

Celebrating holidays, particularly Christmas, has always been a significant part of our family life, and the stories surrounding Christmas through the years are also reflected in these pages.

My Voice will introduce readers to a warm, wonderful family and the funny situations that are a part of life. Hopefully those of you picking up this book will see your own lives reflected here, and you will share a smile with your loved ones.

Acknowledgments

I want to thank my husband, Mike, and our son, Matt, who have encouraged me over the years to write about the life stories we've shared. You two mean everything to me.

Thanks to my parents, Mick and Marie Mankey, who gave me a childhood of love and support from which I drew time and again as I wrote about the warm and funny moments that are so much a part of this book.

Thank you to my siblings, Mick Mankey and Margaret Timme. You two are a wonderful part of my life and an integral part of these essays.

Thank you, Cheryl Modzelewski, for being my best friend and cheerleader since our playground days in elementary school. We have been there for one another's hallelujahs and heartbreaks over these many years.

I thank you, Maryanne Datesman, for being the visionary that you are. Your friendship and professional knowledge are unequaled, and I am so blessed that you are in my life.

Thanks to Theresa Meacham, artist and friend. From across the sea you agreed to get on board and make this book something more than it could have been without you. Your creative drawings and working partnership have been invaluable to *My Voice*.

I want to thank two of my writing colleagues, Barb Strauss and Graciela Andresen, for holding my feet to the proverbial fire. Without you two, I might still be at the drawing board!

Thank you to John Hecker and Jane Green, two people who have encouraged me throughout the years to keep writing. Your kind words have never been taken lightly, and you have taught me important lessons in perseverance.

I thank my publishing company, The News-Gazette, Inc., and John Foreman, its president, who accepted my very first "Voices" essay. I also thank my skilled project editor and others at the News-Gazette who have worked with me throughout the years, including Denny Santarelli, Tom Kacich and Dan Corkery.

And last but not least, thanks to our cat, Cocoa, who could always be counted on to curl up on my keyboard at the most crucial of times, and to our beloved dog, Dudley, who lay loyal and patient at my feet as I wrote. Good dog.

PART ONE

Just a Dollop

Best of Intentions

Think *I Love Lucy*. Better yet, think *The Three Stooges* minus one. Now you'll have a picture in your mind of our comical yet best-of-intentions recent house projects. Our son had just bought his first home and was away on vacation. My husband and I decided that since it was summer, and we had the time, we would take this opportunity to travel north a few hours and lend a hand at the new house. Our son agreed, saying he could use help with two things: The sprinkler system wasn't working correctly, and his plants would need watering before his return. If we could help with those two tasks, he could handle everything else.

Our first night on the job we tried to close the dining room blinds. Those long, lovely vertical blinds had a mind of their own, and the more we pulled cords and twisted individual blinds, the worse it got. With The Project Man, my husband, taking charge, I gave up and went to bed. Sometime after midnight, my husband woke me—not to say goodnight, but to tell me he had no idea what he had done to the blinds, and first thing in the morning he would have to call someone to repair them. I turned over and remembered our son's words: "All I need help with, Mom, is the sprinkler system and watering the plants." So much for day one.

The next morning I woke early, and after staring at the closed and twisted blinds for a while, I began to investigate other rooms in this new house. I thought having my coffee in the sunroom would be a pleasant way to start the day, so I pulled a sliding door that opens into the sunroom—with no results. (Little did I know that it was just a stubborn, old, in-need-of-some-oil sliding door.) "It must be locked," I thought, and I turned the locking device to open the room. Now it really was locked, and we had no keys to any of the interior doors, since all we needed to do was "check on the sprinkling system and water the plants."

After the blinds incident and the locked sunroom, one would think we had learned our lesson, but just as Lucy and Ethel ventured deeper into their comedies of error, so did Project Man and his sidekick. We tore down paneling in the basement to expose water leaking in through a window, and the next few hours were spent with a squeegee and paper towels trying to contain the wet mess.

Outside the house was fair game as well. Without a pole-saw for cutting dead limbs out of a backyard oak tree, Project Man borrowed our faithful dog's 20-foot stake-out lead, climbed up on the flat roof, lassoed branches (Will Rogers would have been proud) and pulled them down. When that method was no longer useful, he used a 2×4 like a javelin and, leaning forward on the roof, like the winged Mercury, he hurled the 2×4 toward higher unruly limbs, bringing them down with a crash. No broken bones or windows; we were so lucky! Although neither the dog lead nor the 2×4 were in my hands, I knew that I was just as guilty because I was the accomplice in these little fiascos. I could see it now: A judge would issue a restraining order stating that we had to stay away from our son's home when he was not present! From behind his lofty bench, the judge would shake his gavel and say, "Why didn't you just look at the sprinkler system and water the plants?"

Like a chocoholic who craves the sweet treat or a Lay's potato chip fan (bet you can't eat just one), it was too late to reverse our path, and our need to complete "just one more task" was out of control. We pulled weeds, dug out contrary vines, cleaned gutters, interviewed lawn-mowing companies, got a bid from a contractor on a basement remodel, planted flowers, pruned rose bushes, hung pictures, bought new door mats and bathroom rugs, raked the yard and tarred a leak in the roof.

We left for home the third day. I was afraid we might start to build on a new addition if we stayed any longer. The sprinkler system? It's still not working. The plants? They could probably use another good watering about now, but I think we will leave that to the new homeowner.

Downsizing Made Simple

Everywhere I turn recently there are articles, news reports, TV programs and Facebook posts about having too much stuff. It used to be just my mother who had all that stuff, which in truth was really a lot of *my* stuff that she kept. Eventually, the time arrived when I became the proud recipient of my childhood and not-so-childhood belongings. My mom was a wonderful, caring lady who kept all my elementary school Christmas projects, 4-H crafted ashtrays, dance costumes, horse figurines, comic books, prom dresses and so much more. All of that stuff is now taking up room in my house. When you add my husband's stuff (1960s stylish blue jeans, baseball cards, more comic books, boxes of loose pictures destined for inclusion in family albums) and you add to that our son's collections of rocks, seashells, hockey paraphernalia, comic books (there seems to be a theme here) . . . well, you get the picture. It's too much. And just like the snow this winter, it's time for a lot of this stuff to go! Sometimes I can push the thought of dealing with all these possessions to the back of my mind. Recently, however, it has been hard to ignore, because of the attention given to the topic of "stuff." Earlier this month, NPR's Ina Jaffe had a piece on downsizing, the retirement age and letting go of stuff. I turn on the TV and see those scary stories of hoarders and how they can't stop gathering stuff. The time had come to address this issue in my own life, but I wasn't quite sure where to begin.

Then my husband reminded me of his Aunt Blanche, who lived to be 103 and was known for her take on "all that stuff." When her time came, she had only a few essential, precious items that her family lovingly took possession of. Her formula was simple: throw out, discard, pitch, toss 27 things a day. That was it. No gimmicks.

"Just eliminate 27 things," she used to say, "each and every day. It's not a project; it's a lifestyle." I decided to give it a try.

Would I really be able to find 27 things each and every day that I no longer needed to keep? I happened to be standing in the kitchen when the idea of actually starting this ritual struck me, so I initially tackled that one drawer (or maybe two) everyone has that contains rubber bands, twisty ties, expired coupons, chip clips, paper clips, pens, pencils, appliance light bulbs, oh, I could go on and on. I easily threw away 27 things. I turned to the baskets in my TV room that hold magazines and catalogs and did the same thing the next day. I looked in my linen closet at the twin and double sheet sets I never use, and out the door they went to Goodwill. Next, I took on some of my boxes that had been stored for oh-so-many years. Out went my college textbooks. An old table and rickety chairs were placed in a neighbor's garage sale; wind-tattered umbrellas and high-heeled shoes I've long since traded in for Birkenstocks have now disappeared. It seemed that wherever I was in my home, a "27 moment" was near at hand. It really wasn't that difficult. I wasn't committing myself to an entire spring cleaning or overhaul of the basement; I was just paying attention for a short amount of time to a very doable daily task. It began to feel good. It was a cleansing of the soul at the same time that it was a cleansing of the drawer or closet or shelf or room.

Although it occurred to me that I could certainly make some progress if I jettisoned some of my husband's tools gathering dust in the garage, I kept the decision to toss or keep to my own areas of expertise and declared his stuff off limits.

Starting my 27-things-a-day lifestyle over these recent never-ending winter days has given me time to focus. Now with the promise of spring coming, it should be easy to take this habit I'm forming to the great outdoors. It's time to throw away some old garden utensils, fingerless gardening gloves and two-year old bulbs that were never planted.

It's also just about time to deliver the boxes of rocks, seashells and more to our son's new residence. (And I'm still thinking of a creative way to sneak that box of 1960s blue jeans out of the house!)

Friendship Bread

There's something going around, and it isn't the flu. It's the never-ending loaves of Friendship Bread!

One day my sister received some bread and flour "starter" bags from a friend. The starter is batter that has been started from a previous recipe. The recipient then passes on starter batter to other friends when it's time to bake the bread. Baking the suggested two loaves of bread from the recipe leaves approximately four bags of starter. This batter is then passed to other friends, and so it goes on and on.

As I contemplated the whole process, it reminded me of an edible chain letter without the warnings attached, such as "If you break the chain your batter will be lumpy for the next year!"

So, I had this starter. I mushed the bag once a day for the allotted time and baked my loaves of Friendship Bread.

By taking on this task I had helped my sister, my family enjoyed the bread, and it wasn't much of a hassle to mush once a day for 10 days and add the few extra ingredients required.

I then had four starter bags to pass on to friends, and this is where the dough thickens. I called several friends and offered my starter, but there were no takers. Many of my friends nowadays are not well acquainted with their kitchens, let alone taking on the responsibility of "mushing" each day for a week and a half.

I decided to try a different approach. I drove to friends' houses to give the starter bags to them. Now who can refuse a friend as she hands you a starter bag called Friendship Bread? I'll never know, because no one was ever home!

I kept the starter in my car for three days, mushing it diligently and stopping now and then at a friend's home. But never once did the stereotypical moms from a past generation—June Cleaver, Betty Anderson or Donna Reed (the other one)—greet me and accept my bags.

I finally began leaving the starter at houses with a recipe and a note attached. Was it legal? Was this a display of true friendship? Drop the bag and run: The mashed musher strikes again! It was my last effort at passing on a little friendship, or so I thought. A few days later, my phone began ringing. Friends had questions about the recipe, the procedure, the extra starters, the baking and the sequence of events day-to-day. I had unleashed an uncontrollable phenomenon: Friendship was running rampant!

I hadn't talked to so many friends in ages, and I began to realize that it's not just the bread one gives to another—it's the unspoken promise that a friend will be there to answer questions, explain and help out. An extra copy of the recipe? Sure, I can give you one. You forgot to mush the bread on day four? Wow, let's discuss this. What day would the batter need to be baked if you were going out of town on day 10? Well, here's what I would do. . . .

Friendship is a precious thing, and yet time constraints, jobs, careers and busy lives don't always allow us to express our feelings to others. Giving and accepting the bread, working with it, baking it and passing it on are ways the bread activates those friendship connections.

The bread becomes the perfect metaphor. Friends need one another just as the bread is kneaded; both friendship and the bread take time and effort; the warmth of friendship is reminiscent of the warm cinnamon bread baking in the oven. From one friendship can come many friendships, just as from the first starter bag can come many loaves.

There is no end in sight to this Friendship Bread, for there is always batter left to begin again. Perhaps there is something to be said for starting over, starting again, starting here and now. Something is going around out there, and if we're lucky, we might all just catch it!

Today's Cave Drawings
Are Found on the Fridge

Cave drawings dating back 17,000 years, such as those discovered in the Lascaux Cave in France, allow us to study the life of early man. We can surmise what and how this early human hunted for food, what his family structure was like, and what he valued.

Such visual documentation is useful to better understand ancient man. Where are today's cave drawings? Where can we find a capsulized representation, an in-a-nutshell pictorial depiction, of American family life here in this century?

The answer struck me as I stood in my kitchen recently. I came face to face with my own cave drawings—my personal representations of what is important to this family. I was staring at my refrigerator door. It was all there before me in the pictures and posters, the calendars and cards, in all the magnets and memos plastered, taped and stuck on my cave wall.

Life as we know it was represented there in quips and quotes from wise poets as well as kindergartners. What we eat, were we go, whom we love, when we work and play, and how we feel about it all. Politics, religion and fast food stared back at me, and I saw the truth.

The pictures on my refrigerator represented important and loved family members, friends and memories. There were photographs of our son with school friends, hockey friends and his five older cousins. Photographs of the beloved dog and the bewitched cat, both considered members of this family, were there in front of me.

Family rituals and travels were captured in photographs, too: father and son drinking from a clear, cool Vermont mountain stream, and the two of them on horseback at Indian Guides camp some years past.

Important ceremonies and pageants in our life were captured visually as well. My parents' 50th wedding anniversary and the wedding of a childhood friend were both prominently displayed on my cave wall. Faces of loved ones who are no longer with us are there for us to remember each time we approach that refrigerator.

Written artifacts have a place on the fridge, too. An A+ on a chapter quiz, a Jazz Band program and a nephew's recognized art talent speak of what we value nowadays. Two faded newspaper clippings still announce their messages, "Children Live What They Learn" and "What a Parent Can Do to Foster Self-Esteem." On the refrigerator door, school lunches for the month and upcoming high school and Illini sports events are posted. Even an autograph of #53 from some forgotten sporting event has claimed a place on the door.

I don't know if early man needed to record his upcoming appointments, but we cannot escape such things. Notices of doctor appointments, haircuts, dentist visits and social events become part of modern man's collage.

To keep such vital information in clear sight, magnets dot the landscape. What would future historians decipher from such messages? "Is It Friday Yet?" asks one such holder of history. The food pyramid and a Baskin Robbins magnet rest side by side. Wise parables such as "You Are What You Eat" and "The Greatest Hits of Rock and Roll Are Here" keep our lives in full view.

It's true: Someone from the future could indeed surmise a lot about us from a look at our refrigerator doors. It's all there: how we hunt for food, how our families are structured, what and whom we value in our lives. The cave may have changed, but not the contents.

Happy New Year!

Although the official new year won't arrive for several months, in many ways a new year is about to begin. The end of summer and the coming of fall mark the true beginning for various facets of life. For instance, living in a university community means fall is the start of a new year for University of Illinois students, for campus activities and for football games. Churches have "back to church" Sunday in September for summer's absent shepherds and their flocks. The local park districts and YMCA send out their new fall schedules at this time. Fashion experts tempt us with "what's in" and "what's new" in this year's fall fashion look. Thus, we begin in the fall with whatever fashion statement we choose or don't choose to make for the remainder of the year.

If fall activities and fashion aren't evidence enough that a new year has begun, one only needs to turn on the television to be reminded that the new fall lineup is coming soon. Programs that are fresh in the fall are predictable and boring by early spring. By summer, fall's favorite shows are on the clearance rack.

Perhaps the people who experience a more important new year in the fall are our children. Preschoolers, elementary kids, middle and high school students are all beginning a new school year. Who will my teacher(s) be? What friends will be in my class? Will I be able to unlock my locker? What if I miss my bus? Will my mom be home when I get there? Such questions aren't about academics, but they are the types of concerns students have first before individual subject areas are addressed.

A new school year is beginning and, as in January, a new year is a time for resolutions. What if parents, grandparents, friends, teachers and others didn't wait until January but made some "new year's" resolutions as children return to school?

What if the following resolutions were part of this new school year?

- I resolve to start my child's/student's day, every day, with positive words.
- I resolve to get to know his or her teachers/parents at the beginning of the school year and not wait until a problem may arise.
- I resolve to listen actively to what my child/student has to say, so we can build on our conversations together.

- I resolve to respect my child's/student's fears and concerns, although they may not always seem "important" by adult standards.
- I resolve to meet and know my child's/students' friends.
- I resolve to give my child/student transition time when he or she arrives home/arrives in my classroom.
- I resolve to literally and figuratively step onto the same side of an issue with my child/student, so we can work it through side by side.
- I resolve to slow down, take a breath and really enjoy the time I spend with my child/students this school year.

Perhaps it's possible to get a head start on this new year's business. Call it a sneak preview of good things to come. Although some will wait until January to declare resolutions about losing a few pounds and beginning an exercise program, certain resolutions could make this a terrific new year, starting right now.

Murphy's Law

As a speech and language pathologist, I work with children on their communication skills. Often, a child's language problem focuses on his or her inability to express specific language needs. Exposure to the language and daily practice help develop the student's word-finding skills and general language, so "Give me that thing there" becomes "May I please have the small, dark-green crayon next to Mike?"

Empathy for my students' communication delays was recently enhanced when we experienced a week or so of "Murphy's Law" at our house.

First, it was Vinnie the vacuum cleaner. (I name appliances, cars, bikes, fish, etc. It began as something cute when my son was very young, and only one of us in the family has yet to outgrow it.) Vinnie was running just fine, when all of a sudden he began to make sounds of distress. My husband heard Vinnie's strangulating sounds and dashed into the room. "I was vacuuming over there," I told him, pointing, "when the sweeper started making a suffocating sound like this." (I make the universal strained-vacuum-sweeper noise with lips slightly parted while an "r" sound is produced in the back of my throat.)

Without hesitation, my husband laid the vacuum sweeper on its back and extracted a postcard wrapped around the thing underneath where that little piece of black rubber goes. So much for my knowledge of vacuum sweepers, and just the beginning of Murphy's Law!

My little red car, Betsy, was having a terrible time. When I mentioned her problems to my father-in-law (my own personal mechanic), he wanted specific answers. Did I think it might be vapor lock? Had the oil been changed recently? "Just exactly what is wrong?" he finally asked.

I simply told him the truth: "When I step on the gas and expect a 'roooooom' sound, I get 'er-er-er.'" As for vapor lock, what was that? Oil change? I shrugged.

Well, my wonderful father-in-law changed the oil and suggested I buy a better-quality, no-lead gas. "Look for the middle number, such as 89 instead of 87 or 93," he instructed. I went to buy my gas at the new station suggested, and I looked for this numbering system. Three pumps stood in front of me with the numbers 6, 7 and 8 on them. I chose number 7 because it was the middle number. Why it cost more than the other two, I still don't know. Murphy's Law.

A sick vacuum cleaner and car in the same week are enough, but the other day, I was listening to ol' Monstro, the washer, and what to my wondering ears did I hear?

"Well, sweetie, I think there's something wrong with the washer. Instead of going 'swish, swish,' it was going 'hmmmmmmmmm' this morning." I got accustomed to visiting the laundromat for the next week while Dagwood (just teasing) took apart the timer, the transmission (I thought only cars had transmissions) and the motor. He took the motor from my mother-in-law's washer and put it in Monstro, and eureka! (Whoops, that's a vacuum sweeper.) It worked! My mother-in-law went out and bought a new washer, and we lived happily ever after.

Almost. We have a new computer. It is so new that I haven't developed a personal relationship with it yet, and thus have no name for it. Perhaps Jonathon will do, or maybe Granny. The computer was plugged in and working, and then there was a glitch.

An Apple service representative made a house call and listened as I pointed and grunted out the sounds of computer meltdown. "I was sitting at the computer, constructing my first letter, when something inside that part there (see where I'm pointing?) went 'click, click' and then 'beep, beep' and stopped." Problem? Our new computer had a defective part, and the representative had a replacement with him. Oh, joy!

That's about the worst of it. We're not mentioning the gray car or the squirrel-mutilated bird feeder or the clawed patio screen or the dog's fleas. Murphy struck like a fast-moving virus and has moved on. I believe when so many appliances and our two vehicles all suffer simultaneously, it ensures us of good fortune for some time. I'd say we ought to be well-oiled and humming smoothly around here until, oh, just about time for Christmas!

Communication Prescription

I checked my answering machine when I arrived home from my morning walk on a day off. A message from my doctor's office indicated a prescription had been phoned in for me. I called the pharmacy, pressed the requested buttons on my touch-tone phone and left my name and clinic number. A computerized voice told me when I could pick up my prescription.

While I was seated at my computer a bit later, I sent a friend an electronic bouquet for her birthday. No time to call and visit just now. Next, I shopped for a wedding gift over the Internet and had it mailed without ever speaking to anyone. I checked my email, quickly responded to several messages and crossed them off my list.

The phone rang late that afternoon just as I was preparing supper. My caller ID identified the caller, and I decided to get in touch with the person tomorrow when I could simply leave a response on her machine. Too busy to talk right now.

Such an efficient and tidy day this had been. So much had been accomplished at the push of a button or the touch of a key.

At day's end, I remembered a question I had about my prescription. I quickly called the nurse to leave a phone message; I knew her answer would be on my machine when I arrived home from work tomorrow. I had become efficient at communicating by leaving messages and getting on with other tasks at hand. As I prepared to give my name and number and a brief message after the tone, a voice said "Hello." I was momentarily thrown off balance. I stammered as I realized I was talking to an actual person. This was my first such live connection of the day outside my immediate family, and I apologized for my awkwardness as I tried to put my medical question into words that could be used in a real conversation.

Afterward, I began musing about my momentary inability to communicate with a person rather than a machine. People today conduct more and more aspects of daily life by leaving phone messages or through email or online. A feedback loop from message sender to receiver and back again, which is an essential part of communication, is disappearing. In live communication we speak, listen, comprehend, clarify, request and connect. Our character becomes part of the message when we are actually speaking with another person, and eye contact and body language send strong messages far beyond simple words when we are communicating face to face.

Talking to someone in person is often inefficient, but when the very unpredictable nature of communicating in person with others is practiced, our "people skills" are enhanced. Without ever leaving my home or talking with another individual on this particular day, I realized I had completed most of my daily contacts.

Of course I think telephone and computer technology are wonderful and worthwhile, and I want to fill prescriptions, make dentist appointments, fax information and respond to messages in a timely manner. However, I often miss the people.

Perhaps there ought to be a daily prescription suggesting the amount of human contact and communication needed for a healthy life. The "Healthy Life Prescription" could read: Eat a balanced diet; exercise regularly; get a good night's sleep; and talk in person with others outside your home on a daily basis.

Understanding changing communication trends and devices of today is important, but it may not take away the need to reach out and really touch someone.

Fast and Informal Email

I can remember writing letters to my grandparents and sending my parents and friends letters from camp. Grammar rules for letter-writing were taught and practiced in school and then actually applied in real-life situations.

We learned to put capital letters on proper nouns and at the beginnings of sentences. Basic letter-writing punctuation rules were clear and defined: Indent a new paragraph. Use a period at the end of a sentence. Commas separate items in a series and indicate two independent clauses in one sentence, just for starters. Paragraphs contain information on a single topic. New topic? New paragraph.

Nowadays, I don't write many letters, but instead I send and receive email. As the volume of email increases, I have noticed a common thread throughout most of these messages: There is seldom any grammatical structure to them.

Frequently, there are mixed upper- and lowercase letters in the same word. The typical email may begin without a salutation. After all, if you receive email, it must be for you. At the end of the message there is often no "Sincerely" or "Thanks for your time," but instead the sender signs off with an abbreviation or initials. Sometimes I'm "dreed" (no capitals) or "DR" (no time to put in periods).

The body of the message, unlike the old-fashioned letter (sigh), may begin with no indentation and perhaps no capitalization. Thoughts and comments run on from one topic to the next without taking a breath. The lack of any rule-governed grammar etiquette for emails is like dining out in the new millennium—no formal code exists; casual is the key.

Adhering to letter-writing grammar rules in email seems about as popular as adhering to Emily Post's rules for proper placement of the shrimp fork. No one knows or seems to care.

Not only do grammar rules take a holiday in many emails, but spelling seems to be on R&R as well. Like horseshoe pitching, when it comes to spelling rules and email, closeness counts.

So why doesn't everyone use spell-check before sending their email messages? Perhaps we've come to equate email with a Post-It note or a quickly scribbled message stuck on the fridge. Email is a postscript when it comes to formality. After all, part of the reason to use email is because we're all in a hurry, and email is fast and easy. The focus is on the content, not the form.

Just how important is all of this in the overall scope of things? Perhaps not very, but it is a reflection of a societal change that leans toward the unconventional and away from the formal.

A neighbor was talking about email recently in the company of a person just getting started using a computer. "You'll love email," he said. "Of course, my emails look pretty sloppy when they're sent. I should use spell-check and look over what I've written, but I'm usually in a hurry, and it's so easy just to press the 'send' button."

So what would email etiquette look like? If Ms. Watts, Ms. Weed or Mrs. Peabody were looking over our shoulder, they would remind us to take the time to fix that run-on sentence, to delete that misplaced comma, to begin the greeting with a capital letter.

Indeed, email is becoming this millennium's written expression of who we are. And as the art of letter-writing fades fast into the sunset, we are left wanting something—ah, for the crispness of a well-turned phrase, both in focus and in form!

A Time for Families

As we traveled home after a recent family reunion, the always-asked question came forth as the air conditioning in the car took hold and we relaxed for the drive home.

"What was your favorite part of the day?" My son's answer was quick and to the point: "The food!"

Those of you fortunate enough to participate in summer family gatherings may nod your head in agreement; the food is always delicious, and it is always the same.

We've been enjoying our get-together for many years . . . time enough to take me, a baby boomer, from young adulthood to less-young adulthood. I love to cook and bake when I have the time—which is rarely—but I do know how. Still, my mom and her brothers and sisters are the backbone of this picnic. When we first started gathering together, they fried the best chicken, made the most delicious beef barbecue and homemade noodles, and baked the most scrumptious pies and cakes. They still do. Their children (my generation) participate by "filling in" with munchies, side salads, deviled eggs and cookies. The picnic gets more important every year. It is a precious and rare event in these busy times for a large family spread out across the United States to take the time and make the effort to return to the farm area where my grandparents lived.

My husband's answer to my "favorite part" question was one I wouldn't have predicted, but it pleased me. He said spending time talking with my brother, whom we seldom see, was his best memory of the day. The two of them used to work on old cars together in their teenage years. But marriage, kids and careers have taken us far apart in miles. As they shared their lunch and a losing game of horseshoes, they reconnected.

Horseshoe-pitching is a favorite pastime at our picnic, but changes have occurred over the years. We girls may now take part, and several of the ladies in the family did very well in this year's competition.

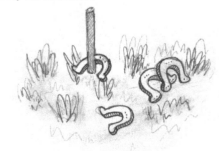

For anyone who can endure the heat, volleyball is also set up in the big open yard next to the farmhouse.

I seem to have become the activities chairperson for the younger set. About eight years ago, it was suggested that the children needed some activities after everyone had eaten and the adults were catching up with each other's news. Having one of the youngest children at the picnic, I decided to plan some events—and no one has fired me yet. I purchased some potato sacks from a feed store for sack races. And although the idea was to give the kids something to do, some mighty hairy legs climb into those sacks for the competition!

A water balloon toss seemed ideal to follow a hot, itchy sack race, so young and old pair up, and we toss ice-cold water balloons back and forth, making the distance between partners greater after each successful throw. When the last pair is left unscathed and declared winners, everyone scrambles to get the rest of the water balloons and pick their favorite personal target.

Our last annual kid event is a good, old-fashioned scavenger hunt. Younger children pair up with an older teenager or a willing adult and search for items around the farm. Because it's the one time a year a youngster may see his great-uncle or his mother's cousin's son, signatures have become a fun part of our hunt. For instance, a child may need the signature of some relative who drove 300 miles for the picnic, or the signature of a country music lover, or a signature from someone who water skis.

"Well, do you want to know my favorite part of the picnic, guys?" I piped up, wanting my turn now. In unison they both replied: "Linda." It's the same every year for me. My favorite part is spending time with a special cousin.

Our story goes way back to when we were little girls from the city playing in our grandpa's hay loft, or finding another litter of newborn kittens behind the barn, or learning how to milk a cow, or swimming in the creek while the guys teased us about water moccasins coming our way. She is my older cousin by just enough years to make me idolize her. Her family moved often during her youth, so whenever we knew they'd be back in Illinois and visiting Grandma and Grandpa at the farm, we'd drive down to spend time with them. She always brought the clothes she had outgrown the season before, and I was always the proud recipient. My mom once took me aside and remarked that if there came a time when I didn't want to wear Linda's hand-me-downs that was all right, for I certainly didn't have to wear them. That time never came.

When I was in high school, Linda came to stay with us on weekends for several years while she finished nurse's training and university course work here in Champaign. All our hopes, our dreams, our disappointments, our secret wishes were shared as only best friends or sisters can share them.

Years have passed. We have realized many of those dreams and have supported each other through a few of life's disappointments. Each year I can't wait to see her again. We try to squeeze a year into a few hours. We take a walk down a hot country road just to find some time to ourselves before we return to the picnic and put on the many hats we wear of mom, wife, daughter, sister, niece, cousin and aunt. Families are wonderful. They are to be cherished and cultivated and enjoyed whenever possible.

Summers: Lazy No More

Are today's summer days the same lazy, hazy, crazy days about which Nat King Cole once sang? Although he certainly made those words memorable, I question their validity today.

I remember my childhood summer days. They were, for the most part, wonderfully lazy, relaxed times spent with friends who lived next door or just down the street. Summers were sprinkled with 4-H camp, Bible school and a family vacation in the Wisconsin woods.

Now friends live on the other side of town, and for younger children a "get-together" with such companions means arranging drop-off and pickup times. Also, summers today come with a frantic rush to get all the family members registered for the right sessions of the right summer activities at the right places and times. Will it be softball Monday and Wednesday nights or Tuesday and Thursday? Will basketball camp conflict with baseball tournament games? Can we fit supper in around swimming and aerobics lessons?

Summers now are a time when families gear up for the busy days ahead instead of calming down after an active school year. I've learned the hard way that one must inquire early about all the summer programs. I now sign us up for July activities while the snow is still on the ground.

Although snow was not present for my son's first Little League game this season, I wore my winter coat and wished I had the blanket of the mom next to me. (Ah, summer can never start too soon.) Little League baseball starts early because it's supposed to be a May–June sport, but if teams keep winning, they become reminiscent of the Energizer Bunny . . . and the conflict with other preplanned pastimes begins.

Nowadays, there is a camp for just about every interest group. Sports camps promise fun as well as appearances by local sports heroes. In this family, baseball camp, basketball camp and hockey camp all have had to fit in to summer's jigsaw puzzle.

With such a flurry of activity, it makes getting up for the predictable hours and schedule of my teaching day seem routine and easy.

What about a family vacation? Families do need a time to reconnect and rediscover each other after a busy school year, and summer has traditionally been that time. Amid the classes, camps, courses, games and gatherings, finding a week or two to get away from it all takes perseverance and prioritizing.

After baseball season, for example, we're "getting away from it all" at a Michigan hockey camp. And there, with all the family together, I plan to get a lot of reading done for my summer school course while I sit in the lobby of the ice arena. It may not be too lazy anymore, but summer is certainly as crazy as the song suggests.

PART TWO

Familiar Faces

Dudley Lessons

"L-o-o-k," I spelled out to my husband this morning as I caught Dudley in yet another irresistible pose. The "l-o-o-k" method at our house means drop everything, don't say a word, don't let him know you're coming, and get over here to see this dog! How do these unwritten rules come about? How did the use of such a word come to have an unmistakable meaning in this household? There are other words we must disguise on a daily basis.

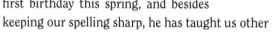

"Do you think he needs o-u-t?" "Are you going to give him a t-r-e-a-t?" "I'm going out to the c-a-r." "Shall we take him to the p-a-r-k?" And the list goes on. Dogs are so darn smart!

The 75 pounder celebrated his first birthday this spring, and besides keeping our spelling sharp, he has taught us other lessons as well. For instance, the Dudster has this way of getting his thoughts together when the world gets a little too crazy for him. He plugs into his "recharging station" for a brief yet important R&R. He may be running in the park with friends, meeting new humans or greeting us after a long (20 minute) absence when he plugs into his recharger by pushing his muzzle between our knees and simply chilling out for a couple minutes. It's his way of taking a break and finding a safe spot in this crazy world. I like this idea, and I imagine we all need a safe spot in which to recharge our batteries before forging ahead once again. What a guy!

Our golden buddy has reminded me, too, of the truth behind the old clichés such as "Don't sweat the small stuff," "Bloom where you are planted" and "It's only a couch." Not long ago, Dudley had an extended play date. Friends were vacationing, so we agreed to have their Brittany Spaniel,

Pebbles, stay the weekend. We quickly found out that there is NO house large enough on a rainy weekend in which a Golden Retriever and a small, spirited, quick Brittany can safely play. I could add that there is no doggie gate high enough, no time-out threats bold enough, no bed big enough and no furniture Scotchgarded enough to withstand the onslaught of the terrible twosome in question. The nimble Pebbles leaped over the doggie barriers we had put in place when we found out rain had been predicted for the entire weekend. Dudley followed the wench by crashing through the barriers of chairs, ottomans and tables as if they were a test constructed for his dexterity! This could have been a humorous moment . . . in someone else's home.

Dudley has opened up new horizons for me. Before Dudley, my shopping world was predictable. Groceries and household and miscellaneous items were all purchased pretty much at the same two or three places conveniently located nearby. Now I have learned to go out of my way to find yet another greeting card with a Golden Retriever's picture on it. As embarrassing as the confession is, I must admit that we have now resorted to buying inappropriate greeting cards just for the adorable Golden Retriever on the front. The rule is now "forget the sentiment, go for the picture!" On my birthday, I received a card with the message "Heel" inside. My husband in turn received a Father's Day card from Dudley wishing "Happy Birthday to My Grandpa." We are shameless! I have searched for dog treats hither and yon, have driven out of my way on road trips to find a new dog toy, and have traveled online to infinity and beyond to research the best food choices for our pal.

Dudley can sit quietly, stay in one place for long periods of time and come when called. He can "take it" and "leave it," and he understands "all done." I'm still working on such lessons, but I've got a great teacher!

I Know a Lady. . . .

I know a lady who was born the middle child and oldest daughter of eight—a responsible girl who cooked, cleaned and cared for her younger siblings when she wasn't helping with farm chores.

I know a lady who made her own long white taffeta wedding gown and bought a single bus ticket from Central Illinois to Texas to marry the young Air Force lieutenant she loved. I know a lady who on each anniversary still slips into her wedding gown, lights her once-tall ivory tapers and spends the evening with that same man. I know a lady who said good-bye to her husband as he shipped out for duty in the Pacific leaving his young, pregnant wife behind. I know a lady who played the single-parent role for the first nine months of her son's life, until WWII was over and she and her handsome pilot-husband were reunited.

I know a lady who baked the traditional homemade angel food cake and planned a birthday party for her 5-year-old daughter only one week after a second baby daughter was born—this lady who has always made each member of her family feel special, for what is important to each of them has always been important to her. I know a lady who thought Elvis Presley wiggled too much and asked her son to watch *The Ed Sullivan Show* from another room if he had to "move that way." I also know a lady who bought her son his first pair of white buck shoes.

I know a lady who stayed up late at night to finish sewing pink feathers and green sequins on Thelma Leah Rose dance costumes for her two daughters. She would stay backstage at the Virginia Theatre the night of the dance recitals, calming and entertaining excited, young, would-be stars.

I know a lady who didn't drive, so she and her girls took the green Short Line downtown on Saturday mornings to shop at W. Lewis & Co., Robeson's and other locally owned department stores.

(I know a lady who secretly took driving lessons and surprised her family one day as she backed the two-toned green 1952 Chevy out of the small, one-car garage.)

I know a lady who taught her 10-year-old daughter how to cook a complete family meal and bake a cherry pie with the patience and love that made a child believe in herself and know that she could not fail. I know a lady who listened and consoled her children when their young hearts got broken—a lady who changed sadness into serendipity and calamities into carnivals!

I know a lady who sent her son off to Vietnam, one daughter to Finland and another away to college all in the same year. I know a lady who always made home the best possible place to be.

I know a lady who went back to work when her children were older and was a high school secretary for almost 20 years. (I know a lady who sees men she knew as boys back then and calls them all by name and holds only good memories of each and every one of them.)

I know a lady who taught her children and teaches her grandchildren to find the good in other people and to speak kind words and share kind deeds with friends and strangers alike. I know a lady who is known far and wide for the most delicious pecan tarts, known as "tassies," ever baked; the smell of their rich butter crust and sweet brown sugar middle cooling in her warm kitchen is a familiar and welcoming scent to all who enter there.

I know a lady who gently and lovingly cared for her 100-year-old mother and made her days brighter with the many little things that are really the important things. I know a lady who brings fun and laughter to a couple's retirement years by always looking for the best in every stage of life.

I know a lady who lives and practices the principles of a happy, fulfilling life—the kind of life that others pay dearly to learn about in books and classes and through counselors and therapy.

I know a lady who is celebrating Mother's Day with her very lucky family today.

Happy Mother's Day, Mom.

A Little Responsibility

For several years now, our son has wanted a paper route. My objections have always been that he'd have to get up so early on winter weekends, Sundays are already hectic around our house, and after-school activities are bound to conflict some afternoons. Thus, a paper route just hadn't been a priority to my way of thinking. Both my husband and son, however, have been resolute in their belief that such a responsibility is character building and should be something sought after, not objected to, in today's society and by today's youth.

"Wasn't it true that Uncle Mick had a paper route when he was growing up and that you helped him, Mom?" That was the question I was recently asked when we revisited this family dilemma. My brother did have a paper route when he was about 12 years old, and yes, I helped him with it from time to time. Such memories are good ones.

I recall one summer back in the mid-1950s. If I hadn't pestered him much that particular day, my older brother would let me help fold evening papers. Those were the days when the local paper was small enough to fold bottom edge to middle, top edge down and just barely lapped over. Then the left side was folded to the midpoint, and the right side was folded and tucked inside the adjoining section. If folded correctly, one ended up with a neat six-inch square that could be tossed through the air and onto a front porch or step . . . with some practice.

There were the two of us, sitting cross-legged on the big front porch, papers stacked high and the tedious task of paper-folding moving itself into a sort of rhythm. "Bottom edge to middle, top edge down, left to right, right to left, tuck, and start again." I would try my very best, never minding the black news print all over my hands, my legs and on the tip of my nose. Once in a while, Mick might say that I could sure fold a lot of papers for a little kid sister. Of course, such comments brought star-studded results, and with fingers flying, I would think yet again, "Bottom edge to middle, top edge down, left to right, right to left, tuck, and start again."

After folding papers I would beg to go with Mickey on his route, but his answer was always the same. This route was his responsibility, not a time to play. Besides, he needed to concentrate on his delivery. Like a pitcher winding up on the mound, Mick prided himself in taking that six-inch square paper, aiming it precisely where the customer wanted it, and with a snap of his wrist, he would deliver it in just the right spot.

Then one day everything changed. A problem had arisen on Mick's route; a problem that had four legs, eight pounds of muscle and the same amount of meanness . . . and no leash! "Trouble," as my dad had so aptly named that loud-barking, teeth-baring canine, and Mickey's paper route were the topic of many supper-table discussions one summer. Various suggestions were mentioned, but back then there were no leash laws, Dad wasn't home from work when papers were delivered and Mom didn't drive. Short of giving up the route, no one seemed to have a solution. And then, I had an idea: If I could come along on the route, I could ride ahead and distract the beast. As Trouble chased me on my bike, Mick could get close, aim, snap and we'd be on our way. Now Mom and Dad knew how much I liked animals, and that of their three kids, I was the one always bringing home a stray dog or cat. So, with some reluctance and yet with pride at an offer of such responsibility on my part, they agreed Mickey and I could give it a shot.

And what a shot it was! Why in no time at all, we had it down to a science. We approached the enemy's camp together. At our first sighting of Trouble, I'd ride like crazy past the house, with the predictable predator snapping at my heels. Mick would then approach the houses on that block, firing one after another of his award-winning paper pitches right smack-dab where he planned them. Hollering with delight as if he had just hit a bull's-eye, after the last house, I would then shake my menacing mongrel, double back, meet up with Mick, and talk about our victory all the way home.

It was true; that paper route taught us responsibility, and responsibility is character building. Perhaps, just perhaps, I need to rethink some of life's present priorities.

Dad's Day: Thanks for the Memories

A few years ago, the topic of conversation among family members was Dad's approaching retirement. Dad always has supported his three children's dreams and ambitions, and we wanted to be there for him as he made important decisions about the retirement years ahead.

Dad always has been active, so we began by thinking of some of the activities he enjoys. He is an avid golfer, and he bowls once a week. He loves baseball and occasionally throws a fishing line out into the lake. He and Mom are also walkers, and they walked long before it became fashionable to do so. It has amused us that Dad never comes home empty-handed from those walks. He is constantly picking up sticks and twigs and bringing them home to use as kindling in their big old wood-burning fireplace. You can hear that fire crackling even on a summer's morning, when Dad will tell you that he's just getting the chill out of the air, or on a summer's evening when the night air is as cool as the day has been hot.

With this in mind, someone suggested that Dad could make walking sticks. He liked the idea, and because his name is Mick, his business could be called "Mick's Sticks." It wasn't long before he set up shop in the basement at home. But fumes from the varnish Dad used to seal the wood soon had the whole house smelling like paint thinner. His business partner, Mom, suggested he move his stick business to the old garage out back.

A few years later, it's a predictable sight to stop by and see him at work on his sticks in that little one-car garage with the gravel floor. The garage smells of musty wood and of fresh-cut grass that still clings to the wheels of the lawnmower after a recent mowing. Sticks line the inside walls of the garage in various stages of their development. Some stand ready for debarking, others have been sanded with coarse- or fine-textured sandpaper, and still more stand off by themselves until the wet, sticky varnish dries.

Dad's workstation is a worn-out lawn chair; his business attire, an Illini cap and an old cobbler's apron . . . even though a bright, new, red apron with a caricature of a Mick's Stick hangs on a nail nearby. His workbench is a little wooden table from a child's playroom of long ago, ready with swatches of sandpaper, paint brushes and small containers of polyurethane.

Dad's thick, white, wavy hair stands out as he bends over his work. He may be debarking a stick by hand, or sanding it just so, or methodically sealing the wood with one last coat of sticky varnish.

Watching his hands at work, I remember thinking as a little girl that Dad had the biggest veins popping out on the backs of his hands when he put a worm on my fishing hook or wrapped his big hands around mine to show me how to swing a bat. It's a comfortable sight to see those same strong hands crafting these sticks.

And all the time he works, he whistles. He whistles familiar tunes played on a portable, paint-splattered radio he keeps by his side. As I was growing up, whenever I wanted to know where Dad was I would stop, stand still and listen for his whistle. And now that I'm grown with a family of my own, it's nice to feel I'll always know where my dad is. I'll lean on my Mick's Stick for support . . . and listen.

Happy Father's Day to all dads who have given their own special memories to their children.

A No-Win Situation

It always starts the same way. Last week I bought a pair of jeans. "What do you think of these jeans?" I ventured.

"Fine," he said. A safe answer, he thought. Did he not realize this was just the beginning?

"Fine in what way? Don't you think they're a little too roomy in the thighs and seat?" I asked.

"No, they look fine to me," he replied.

"Do you mean they don't look roomy in the thighs and seat? Do you think they're tight in those areas? Does it seem like I'm trying to look younger by wearing them so long?" Was that sweat appearing on his forehead as he met my barrage of questions?

"Honey, no really, I *don't* think they're too tight in any one area. And I think you look your age, so leave the length as it is." The end of the discussion? Not by a long shot.

"What does 'any one area' mean?" I quizzed. "Do you mean they look too tight in other areas? Do you really think I look my age in these jeans? Not even a little bit younger? I don't think you like these jeans. I think I'll take them back. What do you think?"

Those transitional clothes between seasons are the worst. On the one hand, I feel so ensconced in the wardrobe that I've worn for many months that I hate to replace it. On the other hand, I can't wait to get into something new and fresh!

Unfortunately, the new season's trappings don't have time to get acquainted with my body before I have to start wearing them. "Does this jacket look all right with this outfit?" I asked recently.

"Do you mean the color?" He takes a stab.

"Color? Is there something wrong with the color?" I query. He realizes it wasn't a color question and expeditiously tries to move on, so as not to get hung up on a discussion of my ability to color coordinate my own wardrobe.

"Did you wear that jacket with the same outfit last year?" he inquires as he tries to side-step the issue, although he hasn't the slightest idea what the issue is!

"Don't you remember this outfit? How could you not remember this from last year? I wore it to the graduation ceremony, and the progressive dinner and Dad's retirement banquet. I wore it practically every time we went out. I haven't bought a new jacket for decades, it seems!" He realizes that this has now crossed over into the I-can't-wear-this-old-thing-one-more-season subject. How did it happen? Which comment was it that led me straight out of my closet with last season's clothes and into the nearest mall to buy new fashions?

I must admit that I sympathize with my husband to a certain degree. I respect his opinion. I am asking legitimate questions that require an answer from someone who really knows me. I just don't understand, however, why he can't get it right!

I had a hair appointment scheduled recently, and I thought perhaps a different approach was called for after our track record of communication foofaraws.

"I'm getting my hair highlighted today, and when I come home I hope you say you like it, okay?"

"Let's practice," I teased. "Hey, Mike, I got my hair highlighted; what do you think?"

"I like it," he answered on cue. Perfect! Perhaps this was the way we should work out such matters in the future.

As I came through the door after my hair appointment, he was there to greet me. "Hey," he smiled. "I see something has been highlighted!"

Oh well, that's close enough.

Five Reasons Not to Get a Dog

Empty-nester friends contacted us recently to ask our opinion: "Should we get a puppy?" While their three children were growing up this family always had a dog, but that was some years ago, and now they were needing some advice. My husband and I are empty-nesters as well, and just like our friends, we had a dog for many years. Kind, irreplaceable ole Captain and our son, Matt, grew up together. When we said good-bye to Captain after 16 years, we decided that he was a once-in-a-lifetime companion, and we were one-time dog owners. Years passed; Matt grew up, and something was missing. Then, after six years of just going about the business of coming and going, we had a change of heart. Mike and I decided two years ago to welcome a new puppy into our lives, and nothing has been quite the same since!

When our friends first asked the question, "Should we get a puppy at this stage of our lives?" I was ready with lots of advice. For instance:

1. A dog must be walked rain or shine, I reminded our friends. Dudley, our Golden Retriever, knows which one of us is the early riser, and his wet nose nudges me good morning as reliably as an alarm clock. Our friends need to think about the following question: Who wants to exercise daily with a companion who never complains about the weather? Who wants to meet and get to know some great neighbors out walking their own dogs on a daily basis?

2. A dog requires vet visits and food . . . lots of food, I tell them. Dudley was a cute, small, furry ball for about a minute, and then quickly became a big guy who now expects to be fed good, nutritious dog food twice a day! Who wants to spend money on a member of the family who loves you unconditionally when you could be getting more cable channels or a smarter smart phone?

3. A dog requires training, and this takes time. If trained properly, I told our friends with the wisdom of one who has been there, then the results will be a quiet, well-behaved pet who sits obediently when visitors drop by. (Otherwise, like some people I know, you will have a noisy, lovable clown when visitors drop by . . . oh well.)

4. Traveling is difficult. Who wants to travel with a dog? We never traveled with our first dog, but decided to give it a try with the Dudster. We traveled over 10 hours to take Dudley back "home" to Minnesota to reunite

with his mom and siblings. The experience taught us that traveling with a dog certainly isn't like traveling with children. Why, a dog just wants to sleep in the back seat (or crate), acts happy no matter how many wrong turns you take or where you're headed, eats when you feed him, "needs to go" when you tell him, and licks you behind your ears while you're driving! They better be prepared!

5. A dog sheds hair everywhere! Who wants to sweep, Swiffer and vacuum when all you get in return is someone who is always happy to see you, misses you when you're gone, warms your feet at night, enjoys the same TV that you do, and looks at you with the biggest, most soulful eyes that say simply, "I love you"? Indeed.

Needless to say, we had a thing or two to say as we advised our friends. And, needless to say, they paid little attention to my "list of five" and welcomed their Golden Retriever puppy, Tupelo Honey, into their home recently. Mike, Dudley and I couldn't be happier!

Boomers in the Kitchen

"We baby boomers are different than your generation," I told my dad. "For example, couples today spend more time in the kitchen together than you and Mom did." And so began my explanation of how my husband and I are often side by side preparing the evening meal and generally making the culinary experience a cooperative venture. And it is true, my husband is very willing to help in our meal preparation. It is also true that we handle kitchen duty just a bit differently.

For instance, when my husband makes a salad, he finds and adeptly handles speciality utensils that I never knew we owned! Such utensils cut, dice, peel, slice, scrap and chop food into the most incredible shapes and sizes. I'm amazed at the creativity that can go into slicing carrots. (I've also learned that more than one side of a grater can actually be used.) I'm partial to stirring veggies, fluffing rice, and turning meat with the same spoon. One utensil, one thing to wash—that's my motto.

Some nights I walk into the kitchen without an idea in the world about what will appear on my family's plates in the next 30 minutes or so. As the restless fans jeer, "What's for supper?" or "I'm hungry now" and, every mom's favorite, "There's never anything to eat in this house," I begin scanning the cupboards, fridge and freezer for little food morsel mysteries that might be tucked away and about which I have momentarily forgotten. Somehow or another, a meal is prepared, we sit, we eat.

When I'm off KP duty for that particular night, the scenario might go something like this. The latest issue of a new health food magazine is scanned for a healthy alternative dish for that night's meal. Nevermind that it is already 5:30 p.m. when Chef Tell begins to peruse his palate-pleasing pages. (Personally, I have always secretly hoped that by just subscribing to so many health-conscious periodicals my cholesterol level would drop and my sodium intake could be ignored. Surely I don't have to read them and use the recipes, too!) After he decides on the perfect dish, shops for the unusual but healthy ingredients and prepares the meal, we are eating at about 8:00 p.m. Is it always delicious? Of course.

It's not just sharing the responsibility for the supper preparation, but sharing the working space as well that has its own individual quirks. Now I know I shouldn't complain as we stand there together creating a meal, but deep down I'm secretly saying, "I don't slice carrots, I shred them; I always use this small cutting board not that huge one when grating zucchini. I leave the lettuce in bigger pieces for salads. I always pare an apple into eighths . . . and leave the peel on!" Instead of speaking out on such issues, I take a deep breath and remind myself of what I had recently told my dad: In the baby boomer generation, husbands and wives share more tasks. After all, my husband isn't reclining in a La-Z-Boy watching television; he's not asleep on the couch waiting to be called to dinner; and he's not glued to the computer as he surfs the Internet. Still, it's hard to relinquish control of "my kitchen turf" when we're both wearing the chef's hat for that evening and wielding paring knives, too, I might add.

We also cooperate with kitchen responsibilities on nights when I'm in class or have a late meeting. Although I like to prepare a meal on half of one countertop, using a recipe with at least 50 percent of the ingredients on hand, that just doesn't work for everyone. When my husband cooks, he doesn't begin until the cabinets have been double-checked to make certain we have all the ingredients called for in a recipe and in the right amounts. (Talk about excessive!) Every inch of kitchen counter space is used, and all those fancy gadgets come back out to assist the chef. I appreciate his help, and yet there remains that voice inside that whispers, "Don't rearrange my wax paper/twisty-tie/coupon/rubber band drawer while you're waiting for your almonds to caramelize!"

Baby boomer couples are in this thing together. We boomer wives wanted our husbands to help out at home, just like many of us help the family outside the home in jobs and careers. And yet I turn into Beaver Cleaver's mom when the supper hour approaches, no matter how rushed and disjointed the evening is. Perhaps I'll buy somebody a La-Z-Boy for his birthday!

One Family's Way of Giving Thanks

We recognize Thanksgiving in various ways. In the classroom we talk about the hardships that the Pilgrims endured, the Native Americans' way of life, and the influence both had in our country's history. Our churches hold religious services to give us time to reflect and be quietly thankful. But the fondest memories of so many of my Thanksgivings come together each year at the best place of all: Mom's Thanksgiving table.

Each family member plays a significant part in the day's celebration. My mother plans and executes much of the menu: turkey, yams, oyster dressing, mashed potatoes, cranberries, scalloped corn, pumpkin pie, chocolate cream-pie tarts and her specialty, pecan tassies.

Mom always sets the big formal table several days in advance. She places all the serving dishes on the table and puts labels on each and every one, so she knows exactly what food goes where in those rushed minutes before everyone is called to the table. She always asks the youngest grandchild to make the place tags for guests. This way, everyone participates.

For his part, the patriarch watches football until summoned to carve the beast. Dad has us all gather at the Thanksgiving table and hold hands as he leads us in a prayer. These prayers are always very personalized and mention family happenings and accomplishments in the past year for which we are all thankful. (Dad's prayers are not without their humorous moments, such as the year he mentioned a new daughter-in-law at the table and called her by an old girlfriend's name!) Dad also places a lottery ticket at everyone's place, so we each have a chance once a year to become a millionaire.

We all claim responsibility for originating the idea right there at the Thanksgiving table that Dad should make walking sticks for a hobby when he retired. He and Mom did a great deal of walking together, and he often spotted a favorite stick along the way to bring home. It has become his retirement hobby since its inception that Thanksgiving Day several years ago.

My sister (who, by the way, made and has worn an authentic Pilgrim's outfit in years past) probably has the biggest heart of anyone gathered for the feast. She always extends an invitation to others to join our family for that special day. We've enjoyed the company of Chanute servicemen, University of Illinois students, new families in the community or those who just don't have others with whom to spend the day. The table always seems to accommodate just one more guest.

My brother must travel the farthest, so, of course, we're all anxious to hear when he has arrived safely at Mom and Dad's. He and his wife bring four college-aged sons who enjoy their grandmother's home cooking as all good grandsons do.

My role is to bring us all together with a special poem or a new game to play. Last year, everyone had a different famous person's name pinned on his or her back. Each of us had to ask questions of everyone else until we guessed our famous person's name. We found we ate more slowly and enjoyed more time at the table by having a conversational gimmick.

Past ideas include each guest choosing a letter from the expression "Happy Thanksgiving" and sharing something for which they are thankful that begins with their letter. I've also brought a microphone and speakers and had all the family members sing "Gabby the Gobbler" or "Little Johnny Pilgrim." This year my contribution is to ask each family member and guest to perform one random act of kindness during the week of Thanksgiving and to share that good deed with the rest of us on Thanksgiving Day.

After the meal, young and old alike retire to the family room for charades. I'm not sure if we've ever kept score, but I am certain that we all have a wonderful time laughing together. Thanksgiving is a wonderful holiday. No gifts to buy, no wrong sizes or colors, no last-minute decorations to worry about. People gather together and share some of themselves and a delicious meal.

Then, after the last dollop of whipped cream has been dropped on the final piece of pumpkin pie, we all go home reminded how thankful we all should be for the good things in our lives.

The Memory Box

Last year for Mother's Day, my brother, sister and I gave our mom a memory box. Inside the box were slips of paper, each with a special memory from one of us. These weren't sentiments such as "Thanks for paying for my college education" or "Thanks for teaching me right from wrong," although both are examples of the many things that mothers do for their children.

Her memory box was filled instead with those seemingly unnoticed, day-to-day things that occur during a lifetime between mother and child. We decided not to assume that Mom knew the way we felt; we wanted to tell her. When we gave our gift to her, we shared the hope that she would look in the box occasionally whenever she wanted to be reminded of some memories that her children held dear. We also told her we would be quietly adding to the box throughout the coming years as new memories were forged.

There in the box were thank-yous and statements such as "I remember you made my butterfly net for me and helped me with my butterfly collection;" and "I remember the mud house I built in the backyard one summer. You never said a word about the horrible mess and even praised my results;" and "I remember how wonderful your pink hand lotion smelled when you would lean down to kiss me good night years ago;" and "I remember the two of us visiting college campuses during my junior year and how wonderful those long talks were in the car as we traveled."

To mother is an active verb. Because moms are busy on a daily basis attending to their children's needs, they may not realize the tremendous impact the little things they do have upon their children. To mother means giving hugs, kissing scraped knees, cheering from the bleachers, practicing multiplication tables and reciting bedtime prayers together. Such things are done each day because moms love their children. Just as true as children grow older, moms are adjusting wedding veils, miraculously quieting crying grandchildren and sharing cooking tips while they continue to give hugs and kiss life's little scrapes.

Thank-yous to moms can happen everywhere and at any time. Last Thanksgiving, after many years of enjoying the best homemade turkey gravy ever at my mom's table, I finally took the time to watch and listen to how she made it. I would have put that thank-you into today's box.

This past Easter I was waiting for Mom to call and tell me about Easter dinner plans at her house for all the family. Each year the family gathers at Mom and Dad's after church, shares a delicious meal and then hunts for Easter eggs in the yard. It has never mattered whether one is 8 or 80, the hunt has always been a highlight of the day. With Easter only a week away, I still hadn't heard from Mom. I called and asked what our plans were going to be. She sweetly suggested that maybe it was time to start some new traditions and that she and Dad had no particular plans for the day. The gavel had been passed.

After a few quick calculations, I invited the family to our house this year. We had a wonderful time, and I'm so glad she allowed me to share that day with her in my home. I would have put that thank-you in her memory box today as well.

Our mom is not with us now, and we have found that life's tomorrows were only possibilities, not promises. Mother's Day is a good day to remember the little things that moms are always doing, for they are really the important things of life.

PART THREE

Wishes and Wonder

The Truth about St. Nicholas

Christmas is a time of magic. Christmas memories stored away during the year resurface when the first flakes of snow fall or that first familiar carol is heard.

Holiday memories come tumbling forth in no particular order and for no particular reason . . . unless, of course, it is the magic.

Early one December, I remember asking my older brother the unthinkable question. I was hesitant to utter the words aloud, but my wondering could no longer be kept inside. Of course since that time so many years ago, I have come to know the answer. I know without a doubt there is unmistakable magic at Christmas that no one can explain and that we must just believe.

"Mickey," I asked, "is there really a Santa Claus?"

"*Why* are you asking? Don't you believe?" he asked. I told him about the baby doll I had received the year before, the doll I loved most in the world. She had been set out where I could see her the first thing early that Christmas morning. The lights of the Christmas tree gave the room a soft warm glow, and there in the midst of it all was the doll I had asked for from Santa. And what a wardrobe she had!

How busy those elves must have been!

When we gathered up our toys and went to visit relatives at Grandma's farm later that Christmas day, I heard someone say what beautiful clothes my mother had made for my new doll—each one to match a part of my own wardrobe. I hadn't thought about it much as the year went on, but here at Christmastime again such thoughts came back to me. Did Mom make those clothes, or could Santa's elves really perform such magic? How could I be certain there really was a Santa Claus now that this first doubt had crept into my mind? My brother and I decided that we would watch for a sign this year to let us know. To let us know if the magic was real.

The anticipation was horrible. It was wonderful. And then, it was finally Christmas! The scene repeated itself as it had in years before and as it would continue to do each and every Christmas we children spent growing up in our loving family. Sometime before dawn Christmas morning, we slipped out of bed. The brightly lit fir tree stood casting a wonderful spell on the toys and gifts below. There around the tree was the train set my brother had wanted. It was on the track and ready to go. But there was something wrong. Several of the train cars were a bit rusted.

Mickey and I had both noticed it. Santa wouldn't give a child a second-hand train set. Could this be the awful proof we were looking for and yet hoping not to find?

When my parents awoke and joined the excitement, Mickey showed them the rusted spots on the cars. It was after this day that I knew the truth. My mom and dad were surprised, but they made sense right away of what had happened. Santa had no doubt dropped the train from his sleigh full of toys, and by the time he and his reindeer had found the little train in the snow, it must have rusted.

Of course! Of course, I said to myself. Why hadn't I realized that? That year was truly one of the very best Christmases, for it was the Christmas that made me believe again in the magic of this season—a magic that revisits us each year if we only let it.

A New Beginning

This is not a Christmas advertisement. It is not a recommendation for one to go out and acquire a pet for the holidays. It's just a story, with a bit of Christmas spirit attached, about a Golden Retriever puppy named Dudley.

As empty-nesters, our daily lives had settled into predictable patterns around here. Up at the same time, out the door on schedule, home in the evening, dinner in front of the TV, to bed and up again. About a year ago, I decided that the answer to this boring predictability that had taken hold was to get a puppy. Everywhere I looked I saw adorable puppies. It seemed the majority of friends in the neighborhood either had a dog or a new puppy. I was hooked, and I began two quests. The first quest was to make calls, search the Internet, talk with good pet owners and find out as much as possible about getting a new family member that was the right fit for us. The second quest was to talk my husband into this desire of mine to have a dog.

My arguments were measured and planned. A dog would mean we would exercise more. A dog would give us companionship and stir things up a bit in this quiet house. A dog would give us a shared interest. Slowly and methodically both quests were realized, and Dudley became a reality. He entered the picture a few months ago, requiring, well, everything from us.

We read book after book about training the new puppy; we researched articles online; we scientifically investigated every ingredient in the "best" dog foods—and we thought we were prepared. But you can't be prepared where your heart is concerned. And Dudley stole our hearts.

We knew a new puppy would mean getting up during the night. It would mean being available, regardless of busy schedules, to make sure he was exercised during the day. It would mean crate training, grooming, vet appointments, puppy classes and creating socialization opportunities. We agreed to do this because Dudley was to be the answer to our predictable lives. He wasn't the answer, however. Instead, he became a catalyst to the future.

I now look forward to walks in new surroundings, visits to out-of-the-way parks, travels to lakes and getaways where it's just perfect to take our young companion. We missed the "play date" generation with our son, but not so with Dudley. We now make play dates with a coquettish Brittany named Pebbles. Dudley has had play dates with an older, wiser Golden named Peyton and backyard play dates with Flicka and Arthur. Dudley is old enough now to run with the big boys like Murphy, Joey, Ruby, Louie and Popcorn in our neighborhood park. And as Dudley's world grows, so does ours. We've met people that we never would have met before Dudley, like Susan and Hogan, the Kennedys and Lexie, Dick and Lucy and many more. Now we look forward to visiting with both dogs and owners throughout the neighborhood and at the local dog park.

Dudley has changed our lives. He's a conversation starter and a laughter magnet. His antics around the house bring smiles and snickers much more often than they bring reprimands. He has created an adventure for both of us as we look forward to an unpredictable, page-turning future. Here at Christmastime, when we give reverence to the past and reach back to touch nostalgic times, a puppy named Dudley has given us a new beginning.

Holiday Highlights

Whatever the name, Christmas pageant, winter program or holiday song festival, these events are a tradition in most schools, churches and youth organizations at this time of year. This is one memory that can be shared by generations of grandparents, parents and children who have participated in such December productions.

I recently attended an elementary school winter program and was seated next to the grandmother of one of the bright smiling faces on stage. The first graders had just finished a multicultural song complete with Orff instruments. (Orff instruments are mallet instruments, such as the xylophone or glockenspiel, that encourage a hands-on approach to music learning.) The white-haired lady next to me leaned over and said, "You know, I played the xylophone one year in my grade school Christmas program, and it was the highlight of my elementary school years." Her comment surprised me. "The highlight of her grade school years?" It's easy to forget just how important such events are in the lives of our children as we rush through this busy season and our generally busy lives. Maybe it's time to remember.

As I listened to contemporary tunes mixed with a dash of traditional favorites about snowflakes tapping at windowpanes and snowmen coming to life, my mind eased back to the days of my own such programs. I can remember standing on the cold, marble school stairway in second grade practicing "We Wish You a Merry Christmas." We had been instructed for several weeks to enunciate clearly, so it didn't sound like "We Wi-shoe a Merry Christmas." I concentrated on that line so fervently that I no doubt made my teacher's worst fears come true!

My fifth grade year I stood across from Billy. As we sang in a stuffy, crowded upstairs hallway packed with kids and parents, he started to look a bit green. I was aware of his eminent condition and prayed that an adult would rescue him before the inevitable. My prayers were answered in the Old St. Nick of time, and on went the show.

As third graders, we lined up and marched to our designated spots on the rafters. I was walking next to Sandy when she turned to me and remarked, "I know how to spell Czechoslovakia." I don't remember why she said that; perhaps we had been studying geography (you know, George Elliot's old grandmother rode a pig home yesterday). Whatever the reason, I worked on the spelling of Czechoslovakia throughout the program and have always credited Sandy and a little wholesome competitive spirit for my success at spelling that most useful word.

Perhaps one of the elements we as members of the audience enjoy so much about these holiday/winter programs is their live production vulnerability. We see our children in all their fresh-faced innocence, smiling out at us and searching for mom or dad or grandma and grandpa. The slick musical extravaganzas don't have the same appeal as these innocent, low-budget, child-centered productions.

Last year our preschool and grade school youth at church were the stars of a December musical program. It captured just the right amount of child-generated unpredictability. Toddlers in modest homemade costumes sang "O Tannenbaum" as Christmas garlands fell to the floor behind them, and two glass ornaments attached to the garland shattered . . . off cue. Everyone loved the show!

If we should doubt how memorable such an event may be, we need only remember the words of the lovely lady seated next to me at this year's program or revisit our own youth and be touched again by such magical times.

Lasting Memories of Christmas Giving

At Christmastime, we share with our children the age-old axiom that "it's better to give than to receive."

"Well, Mom, did you think it was better to give than to receive when you were a little girl?" my son asked recently. I told Matt I needed to think about the question.

Christmas was always a wonderful time when my brother, sister and I were children. I remember my brother waking me early on Christmas morning. His skinny frame masked in his Roy Rogers pajamas, his hair tousled from all those anxious, wakeful hours, he would arise at that secret hour tucked somewhere between midnight and dawn when children can wait no longer. At this moment, I was allowed to be his partner, his confidante. We would tiptoe down the creaking wooden stairs, giddy with anticipation, trying not to wake our baby sister or our parents.

There in our living room, the tall Christmas tree stood with lights twinkling (were they left on by Santa?), brightly colored glass ornaments shimmering and silver tinsel hanging haphazardly over beckoning branches. The tree's unmistakable pine aroma seemed more pungent than usual. Indeed, every part of the picture seemed magnified at that hour.

Santa never wrapped that one special gift at our house; thus, such gifts as a doll or my brother's train set were always placed so we saw them first. Our family's rule was that we could look in our stockings, but no other presents were to be opened until Mom and Dad came downstairs, which was before dawn on many Christmas mornings.

As my brother and I delighted in the trinkets found in our stockings, we huddled together on a floor register to keep warm in our big old house. I remember such moments more vividly than any present I received.

Another special memory comes easily to mind. It all began sometime in the fall when I would start to write our annual Christmas play. My big brother and little sister and I would present a play to our parents, our grandmother and any other relatives and neighbors who were sharing Christmas Eve with us. The play was complete with handwritten programs, costumes, stuffed toys and plenty of practice. Many of our ideas came from the 1952 *Christmas Ideals* book that we have kept to this day. Each year new parts would be added, and other skits, poems and songs remained traditional year after year.

For instance, teddy bears were always dressed to resemble shepherds, with sticks tied in their paws as staffs. They became part of the yearly manger scene with my sister as an angelic Mary cradling her baby doll in her arms. An angel dressed in a white flannel nightgown sang "Away in a Manger" from high on the stair steps. "A Visit from St. Nicholas" was recited to my sister at the close of each year's play.

My brother (all of 8 or 9 years old when our plays began) would pass out programs, change the sets, add comedic relief and be the prop man. One year, as my sister stood in her red and white polka-dotted pajamas wearing a red clown nose and poised to sing "Rudolph the Red Nosed Reindeer," my brother tore bits of toilet paper off the roll and dropped them over the banister for a snowy wonderland effect all around the little reindeer.

As I reminisced about our Christmas productions, I realized I had the answer to my son's question. My fondest memories were indeed about the giving side of Christmas, not just about receiving gifts. It was giving that Christmas play to our family and friends that has always been one of my cherished memories. Magical moments also came from those times shared with my brother and sister, or the sight of our beautiful tree as we crept downstairs, or the memory of our cold toes on the little register, or the sound of quiet except for our whispers in the dark before the Christmas dawn.

Such memories are the kind I wish for today's children. He may not realize it as it's happening, but in the years to come I hope my son knows it can be the giving and not the receiving that makes Christmas such a special time.

'Tis the Season

"'Tis the season to be jolly." Sometimes the "ho, ho, hos" of the holiday season sound more like "woe, woe, woes" with all the hustle and bustle, the last minute everything, and the inability to find a peaceful moment in which to enjoy this most wonderful time of the year. I've learned that keeping things in perspective and celebrating on a bit smaller scale keeps the fun in Christmas for us.

It all started several years ago when we decided to have a holiday open house for lots of new friends in our new neighborhood. The candles were lit, and Bing Crosby was dreaming in the background. Our last task before guests arrived was to light the old wood-burning fireplace. Suddenly, smoke began to fill the room, and we realized we had forgotten to take out the insulation that was stuffed in the drafty fireplace flue when it was not in use. After opening windows and doors without much success of clearing the smoke, I called our guests and postponed the party until a future night. What a beginning in our new neighborhood!

The next year, undaunted by our past calamity, we again planned a huge Christmas open house. Several days before the party, I came down with a strain of flu that literally kept me in bed the entire Christmas vacation. When we canceled, everyone was very understanding . . . but our holiday gatherings were beginning to get a reputation.

The third year I felt great. It had snowed earlier in the day, and everything felt special because of it. Guests would be arriving any minute, and we were once again lighting the fire—only this time in our new wood-burning fireplace insert. All of a sudden my husband shouted out words of pain rather than Christmas cheer. He had burned his hand and wrist in his attempt to get our reluctant fire started. I knew the routine. Go to the phone, and call the party off. But my husband's embarrassment at canceling the party for a third year straight was greater than his pain, so he endured the pain for the evening.

This last year was the year nothing could go wrong. Planning began well in advance, and as the hour approached, we were ready . . . or so we thought. As I attended to last minute details on my list, my husband Mike announced, "We finally did it. Everything is ready except for lighting the fire, and we still have an hour to spare!"

"The party doesn't begin at seven this year; it begins at six," I managed to gasp, "and it's five till six right now!" Just then the doorbell rang, and our first guest arrived. Mike and I stared at each other, and then began running as if in one of those old movies where the characters move in fast-forward motion while the rest of the world freezes. Unfortunately, the only thing freezing was our guest outside. As Mike tied his tie and visited with our guest, I sliced cheese and stirred punch. Suddenly, the doorbell rang again, and without thinking, Mike exclaimed for the both of us, "Oh, great! Another early guest!" There it was. Right in front of guest number one. Those words you can't take back as you look for a hole in which to climb. When the couple at the door came inside, we all began to laugh as Mike and I shared the truth with them about our last minute communication mix-up. Not to worry. Our friends would pitch in, and we'd get everything done before the other guests arrived. I delegated, and they worked. Just when I felt things were under control again, I opened the freezer and found all my tiny green spinach balls waiting to be baked.

After that evening, I decided it was time for me to change my party plans. Family members are going to stop by this year for a holiday brunch, and each person will bring food to share. Mike's thinking of converting to gas logs. I think we might really start to enjoy this holiday thing!

The Message of Christmas

It's time for the message once again. It's time for our senses to be stirred as Christmas draws near. Bells ring it out; choirs sing it out; lights illuminate it; trees, decorations, Santa and brightly wrapped gifts symbolize it. Cookies baking and hot cocoa sipped by the fire assure our taste buds and nostrils of the message. And at long last, December, picturesque in her bareness and calming as the snow falls, completes the scene.

The message is delivered reverently from pulpits, humbly from street corners, warmly from the words of family and friends. It's delivered by various voices and in countless ways to all people who are listening, waiting for the message once again.

Three familiar characters who deliver the message are the classic figures of Ebenezer Scrooge, George Bailey and the Grinch, all of whom come into homes and pass it on each year.

As shoppers get caught up in the hustle and bustle of bargain hunting or searching for that last-minute gift, Dr. Seuss's Grinch pays a visit. He discovers as his heart grows to three times its normal size that it's not the wrappings or the store-bought gifts that give Christmas its true meaning, but the people reaching out to one another.

George Bailey, in the holiday classic *It's a Wonderful Life*, delays his dreams of travel and adventure to do the responsible thing for his family and loved ones. Each year viewers watch George as he copes with the daily stress of his business, his nemesis Mr. Potter, his old home in need of repair and his four wonderfully normal, noisy children. With George's financial predicament and the demands and pace of the Christmas season, it's easy to see how overwhelming life appears to him. Time for the message, this time brought by an angel of sorts. George gets the chance to examine what he knew all along but was too busy with everyday life to stop and see. A renewal of the spirit sometimes just needs a nudge; sometimes it just needs the message delivered again.

In Charles Dickens's *A Christmas Carol*, Ebenezer Scrooge requires three home visits before getting the message. The penny-pinching miser hasn't reached out to his fellow man for so long that he can't see it's simply a matter of attitude. At the end of the story, nothing about Mr. Scrooge's life has changed except his ability to see things differently. Scrooge's transformation from the "humbugs" to the "ah-hahs" of the Christmas season can be seen as he calls out from his window to a youngster running by. "What a beautiful morning," declares Ebenezer as Christmas dawns. His view of the world now is as fresh as the crisp, clean air from his open window. As Scrooge enlists the help of the young boy to run and purchase the big turkey in the nearby butcher shop, he finds humor in their verbal exchange. "What a remarkable boy. What a delightful boy," Scrooge remarks of the youngster as if he is seeing and hearing the people around him for the first time.

The message is simple and clear: The true spirit of Christmas is within everyone's reach, as seen through the Grinch's realization, George Bailey's reaffirmation and Ebenezer Scrooge's reawakening. Merry Christmas!

Celebrating the Holidays:
Such an Annoyance!

The holidays are over. It's a melancholy time for me as I pick up, put aside and pack away Christmas for another year. Christmas items are boxed up and tucked away in closets and attics, behind card tables and golf clubs.

Somewhere between lugging heavy blue packing tubs filled with Christmas keepsakes up our narrow stairway and vacuuming needles, cookie crumbs and several unidentifiable morsels from the furniture and carpets, I decided it was time for a few sensible New Year's resolutions.

We had carpets and furniture cleaned just before the holidays. Entertaining holiday guests had left red punch stains on the carpet, cookie icing between couch cushions, muddy footprints in the hallway and flattened fudge under the ottoman. I resolve not to invite so many friends and family members over next year and to enjoy the peace of mind that comes with clean upholstery instead.

As years pass, I acquire more and more Christmas dishes, keepsakes and memories to unwrap, use and display during the holidays. It takes time getting everything out and more time putting things away. I resolve not to use the good Christmas dishes next year, family keepsakes will stay tucked far away, and old teddy bears will remain in their boxes instead of being placed under the tree.

Two cats and Christmas decorations don't necessarily go together. I had placed votives in bathrooms, hung small ornaments on houseplants and filled baskets with pinecones. The cats teamed together to break a votive on the bathroom floor, knock over a huge green plant to better inspect dainty ornaments placed there, and time and again, they took pinecones from baskets as if the baskets were labeled "cat toys." I resolve not to decorate the entire house next year and to cat-proof rooms as much as possible. Plants can remain unadorned, and bathrooms, bedrooms and foyers will play no part in next year's pageantry.

Lighting the fireplace is a big deal at our house. The entire operation is long and tedious. As we bring in logs from the woodpile, we inevitably track in mud and drop bark chips and miniscule particles of outdoor elements along our trail. The fireplace is cantankerous in our older home, and it takes an advanced degree in fireplace lighting to get it lit and glowing. Needless to say, we don't light it that often. I resolve that next year we simply not light the fireplace at all. That way we'll save on both time and the purchase of wood.

Outdoor lights usually go up the first sunny weekend after Thanksgiving. Unfortunately, this year we waited until a frigid day later in December to unravel the garland, tie the red bows and string the lights along the back fence. During the starkness of winter, the displays of outdoor lights illuminate the landscape and the soul, but I was miserable standing out in the cold, fluffing the garland and securing one more bow onto the fence. I resolve to skip outdoor lights next Christmas and simply enjoy the neighbors' lights instead.

On several occasions throughout the holidays, children visited our home. Some of them literally ran around the house, filling up on sugary treats, gaping at the giant Christmas tree and generally acting like anything but adults. They were demanding more marshmallows in the hot cocoa, more sprinkles on the cookies, more Rudolph and Frosty instead of Windham Hill CDs. Next year I resolve to invite folks over who can appreciate the time it takes to frost homemade cookies just so and who will look at and not touch the ornaments placed ever so carefully on our tree.

There you have it. These few simple resolutions might just streamline Christmas next year and make it manageable. A little less hustle and bustle is what I'm hoping to achieve. Think of it: no more stains on the clean carpet, no more Christmas dishes and keepsakes to put away, no more pet catastrophes, no more fireplace mess to sweep, no more frozen fingers as the outdoor lights are set in place and no more children laughing loudly and getting excited around Christmas.

Stepping back and looking at my planned and predictable Christmas, I suddenly realized I was sterilizing the very things that make the holiday special. Christmas is, after all, sharing time with friends and family, using my mother's, and grandmother's keepsakes, and enjoying our home . . . cats and all. It is experiencing the warmth and the smells that only come from a fire in the fireplace and sharing with strangers the joy of the season by lighting up one's home. Perhaps most important, Christmas is extra special when seen through a child's eyes.

Oh my, I can only hope that this year's resolutions are as successful as my past resolutions to diet and to exercise more. If so, not to worry.

Celebrating Traditions

If ever traditions and nostalgia are acceptable, wide-spread and indeed encouraged, it is during the holiday season.

I vividly remember traditions that made my childhood Christmases so special. When I was growing up, our Christmas tree stood in the same corner year after year. Although Mom wanted to change its location more than once, we kids simply wouldn't hear of it. The same cookies were baked each Christmas season. A few new recipes introduced themselves from time to time, but the three baby boomers in the family still asked each holiday season for the Christmas confections that were really the "traditional" ones. The time to unwrap presents was always early on Christmas morning, and even as we got older and our wide-eyed wonder had been replaced with sleepy-eyed self-contentment, we still arose at the crack of dawn to open presents. When the front room was knee-deep in tissue paper, discarded bows and flattened cardboard boxes, we kids were ready to bundle into the car and head for Grandma's farm. There we shared a festive dinner with cousins, aunts, uncles and friends. After all, it was a tradition.

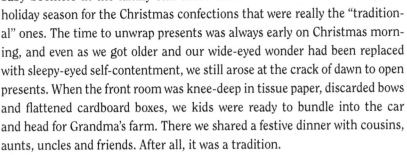

I enjoyed a nostalgic moment during my holiday preparations to reflect upon such childhood memories, and I began to wonder. Are traditions strictly customs handed down from the past generations, or are they dictated as well by our children and the present? As kids, my brother, sister and I certainly seemed to have played a role in what became "traditional" in our family. Perhaps today's children have more to do with what becomes a family tradition than does great-aunt Tillie.

I had wanted to continue some special traditions of my youth in my own family. Despite my planning and attempts to do so, however, the customs and memories of yesterday were transformed by time, place and participants into a look and feel all their own. Some years ago, we bought a tall Christmas tree that reached into the second-story window. We continued that practice for a few years and then decided to replace the big pine with a smaller tree. Our son, who had only experienced Christmas with the tall tree, insisted that we "keep the custom" of having the big tree in the same window. A tradition had begun.

Other traditions in our family established themselves without any of us remembering exactly how or when they began. For instance, when my son was small, Santa's presents did not appear under the tree until Christmas morning. A few years ago, I decided it would look much more festive if presents were displayed under the tree throughout the season. Both my husband and now-teenaged son expressed disappointment that I had not "followed tradition" and waited until Christmas morning to surprise everyone with the special gifts.

Several years ago, my brother was visiting for the holiday, and I invited the entire family for a Christmas Eve brunch. The next year, I did the same. Last year, several family members remarked that they were looking forward to the "traditional" Christmas Eve brunch at our house.

That's how traditions start joyfully and unexpectedly. Perhaps children come to expect a certain look to the holiday scene. Other traditions may simply sneak up on us. (It looks like I'll be having another holiday brunch.) Maybe some of this year's traditions will quietly weave themselves into the fabric of our lives like snowflakes that fall between midnight and dawn, transforming the world we thought we knew into something special and new. It's just possible that a new tradition will begin this year and stay around to become a family favorite.

A Christmas Tribute

This is a Christmas story. It wasn't meant to be. It's just that things aren't always as they seem. In fact, connecting warm thoughts of Christmas to recent events in my life seemed just about impossible.

We walked through the silent house together. We looked at chipped saucers, a small wooden bed with a broken leg, a rocking chair in disrepair. She saw these things with the helpful eye of someone planning for the impending estate sale; I saw things I had known intimately for over half a century there in my childhood home.

With the busy holidays near, my brother, sister and I thought it best to hold the sale before life became too hectic in December. As others took over and discovered our family memories with an objective eye, I poked around the periphery giving information about items when asked, and sometimes sharing unsolicited testimonials. "Hidden treasures" would be found in the grand old home, I was assured by the estate planners. Indeed they were. We found World War II love letters Dad sent Mom from overseas, scrapbooks of my parents' youth, and picture albums of ancestors whose unknown names and faces could now be reconnected with the present. Mom and Dad had also kept memorabilia from our early years including handmade dance costumes from the '50s, prom dresses, a rusted Daisy BB gun and the silver lion with emerald green eyes that appeared on our Christmas tree each year long ago. The disintegrating butterfly wings within my brother's dust-covered collection and the Thanksgiving wishbones preserved from over a score of years were long forgotten treasures as well. Such treasures weren't those the estate planners hoped to find, but then, things aren't always as they seem.

So it went during the fall as we readied for the sale. The marking and tagging of household goods was just one step in the overall journey, for the final destination of this trip would be the sale of the house. This unassuming yet remarkable house was the keeper of everyday memories as well as the treasured memories of past holidays. Thanksgivings found the family seated at the fully extended table enjoying everyone's favorite foods. The games and laughter that accompanied the feast were as traditional as the turkey itself. Easter brought us together for the family egg hunt in which the octogenarians searched for hidden eggs just as competitively, if not quite as quickly, as the youngsters. And then there was Christmas. In the years to come when

I think of that home of my youth, I'll see three wide-eyed children tucked in bed upstairs listening for Santa, and those same children tiptoeing down the stairway before dawn. The spirits of the two parents who made it all possible are intertwined in such memories and breathe throughout the house.

How could all the riches in that home possibly be important to or even be acknowledged by new owners? Such things were on my mind when the phone rang one evening. It was Cheryl. Our friendship went back to grade school, when we had shared overnights in that house, holidays, birthday parties, boyfriend breakups and girlhood giggles. She had news for me, she said. Her daughter, son-in-law and their two small girls wanted to buy Mom and Dad's house. Selling the house then wouldn't be to strangers, but to a young family who would honor the past and put their own mark on the future. New children to tiptoe down those stairs, new traditions to cherish, new laughter and love in that wonderful home. Suddenly what could have been a bleak holiday has all the makings of a very merry Christmas. Indeed, things aren't always as they seem.

Reach Out and Touch at Christmas

Daily life, both at work and at home, is made easier and more efficient by the technological gadgets available today. If I want a new holiday recipe, I go online and find lots of wonderful choices. I can stay in touch with friends and colleagues through email. My inbox is the first thing I check each morning and the last thing I check at night. If I'm running an errand, I'm late getting home from work, I want to eat out instead of cook, or I've decided to do some last minute shopping, the people I need to contact are just a cell phone ring away. If someone wants to take a picture, view a film, or make a call, then he or she probably has the technology to do so right at hand.

How wonderful emails have made staying in touch with servicemen. With computers, a grandparent miles away can now see and talk with a grandchild. Checking in on loved ones, who may need our help when we can't be near, is made possible by computers as well. But, does the use of all these 21st century communication tools make the holidays too easy? The last time I looked, there is no "e" in Christmas. There is an element easing its way into Christmas that may change this special day in December as we've known it. Instead of the familiar "White Christmas," we could soon be singing a different song:

"I'm dreaming of an easy Christmas
Unlike the ones I used to know.
Now the big malls glisten, and we all listen
To hear our cell phone ringing low.
I'm dreaming of an easy Christmas;
I'll be sending emails Christmas night.
May your greetings be faxed, phoned, texted; don't write.
Electronics make Christmas feel so right!"

Stop! Christmas isn't about how easy we can make it. Christmas is about unexplainable feelings that make our hearts glow a little warmer as we reach out toward others in more generous ways. During the holidays, it seems that reaching out and sharing warm wishes with friends, family and co-workers should come so naturally. It might mean putting in some extra time and effort to invite friends over. It might mean planning to travel in order to be with family. It might mean co-workers finding some time to be together away from the proverbial water cooler.

Christmas is the sound of laughter as we share memories. Special memories shared with my siblings after all these years can still bring about some of the best smiles of the season. The years may have twisted the stories and individual interpretations a bit, but the laughter is still healthy for the body and soul. It's the best. Should I just send my brother and sister an electronically produced Christmas letter and be done with it?

Christmas is the smell of cookies baking in the oven and candles burning in our homes. I can still remember the favorite cookies Mom made when I was young. Should we just go online and mail our loved ones cookies this year? It would make things so much easier.

The next generation might say one day, "I remember Christmas when I was growing up. We sent lots of computer messages to people. We called each other and talked because we were all too busy to get together. We received beautifully decorated cookies and cakes sent to us by relatives out east. We always went online and picked out special gifts for family members. It was so easy."

Well, Christmas isn't about being easy. It's essential. It's big. It brings us together like no other time of the year.

So how do we keep Christmas and still enjoy these new electronic portals through which we now move? I've selected my holiday cake and cookie recipes, but now maybe it's time to create a different kind of holiday recipe as well. For instance, one email greeting sent equals one friend I'll invite over for coffee. One online purchase equals one batch of homemade cookies I'll take to a neighbor. Beautiful sacred and favorite secular holiday music can be downloaded on an iPod as easily as rap or hip-hop.

It's not the convenience of all our wonderful communication tools and techno gadgets that will change Christmas. It's forgetting to touch each other. It's forgetting to reach out with our smiles and hugs for strangers and friends alike. It's making that personal contact with another human being that will "keep Christmas." If there's an "e" in Christmas, then maybe it's the way that *each* of us will choose to make this Christmas real.

Christmas Customs: Subject to Change

Christmas has come to be associated with so much more than December 25. It is a time when acts of goodwill happen regardless of religious affiliation; there is unexplainable anticipation in the air; children are ever hopeful; and memories and traditions abound among families. I recently came across this anonymous quote: "Memory is the power to gather roses in winter."

At this time of year, we think about our memories and traditions so much that the words themselves almost become synonymous with the holidays.

Few of us think of change when we are absorbed in Christmas thoughts. Perhaps change, however, is just as much a part of this special season as are all the wonderful memories and traditions. Perhaps change is the power to plant seeds in the winter.

We often change the way we do things. A baby doll was placed in a bassinet under a brightly lit tree, in full view of the young girl who tiptoed down the stairs much too early on Christmas morning. The loving gifts changed over the years, but the scene under the tree essentially never changed. That was then. Now, in my own home, our huge tree is placed in a chilly sunroom that looks out the front room window at the friends and neighbors passing by. Our family gathers not around the tree but around a warm fireplace where gifts and hot coffee await the not-so-early morning risers.

I remember how important it was to my brother, sister and me that holiday traditions remain year after year. From our tree hung the same ornaments that we delighted in seeing each and every Christmas. After moving away from home as an adult, I came home one holiday to find a new look. Mom and Dad had moved the tree to a different room and had hung all new white ornaments on the branches.

To put up our Christmas tree each year, we have begun to use a hook and pulley system because the tree is so tall. In the past it has taken three of us just to get the tree through the door. Then, after several long dysfunctional moments, the tree would somehow be placed in the stand. With the pulley system, the two men in the family can maneuver the tree in place without my helpful suggestions. Indeed, we find new ways of doing things. Such changes are a part of Christmas.

During the Macy's Thanksgiving Day Parade this year, my sister called to ask why there were teenage singing groups performing on just about every float. I had noticed it as well. In the past, the parade's focus had been the giant balloons. Now new interests and elements for the new viewers have been added to the parade, and it's different.

Another tradition we followed for years was watching the local television offering of *A Christmas Carol* on Christmas Eve. Back then it was well after midnight before we would all get to bed. Now we watch a recording of *A Christmas Carol* early some evening before the holiday. We are in bed well before midnight on Christmas Eve. Is that better or worse? It's neither; it's just that our lives and routines change.

Now there is talk of a leaner, non-pipe-smoking Santa Claus. I personally like the jolly, plump ol' Santa who enjoys a good pipe once in a while. Should it come to pass, however, that Santa someday takes on a more health-conscious persona and places a candy cane between his teeth, I imagine I'll adjust.

> "He was cheerful and fit, a right jolly old elf. . . .
> A peppermint cane he held tight in his teeth, and the sweet smell surrounded his head like a wreath. . . ."

The words may be different, but the meaning remains the same. Things will continue to change. Memories and traditions are a wonderful part of the season. So, too, is change as we get ready for the next chapter.

The Night before Christmas

'Twas the night before Christmas, and all through the house,
Not a creature was tweeting or using their mouse.
The stockings were hung by the chimney with care,
In hopes that St. Nick would bring new software.
The children were nestled all snug in their beds,
While visions of video games danced in their heads.
With mama on her Blackberry and I on my Dell,
We'd just contacted friends to connect for a spell.
When out on the lawn there arose such a clatter,
I dropped my laptop to see what was the matter!
Away to the window I flew like a flash,
Tripped over my Mac which I hoped had not crashed.
And there on the breast of the new fallen snow,
Lay the shiny red thumbdrive I had lost days ago.
When what to my wondering eyes should appear,
But a sleigh overflowing with electronic gear.
With a little old driver so lively and quick,
With the click of an app, I knew it was Nick.
More rapid than eagles, his coursers they flew,
With Kindles and iPads and St. Nicholas, too.
And then in a twinkling I heard up on top
Santa's GPS signaling STOP, Santa, STOP!
As I clicked on my phone to text the ol' elf,
Down came St. Nicholas texting himself!
He was dressed all in fur from his head to his toe,
As he tweeted like lightning . . . man, look at him go!
Computers and smart phones were flung on his back,
And he looked like a geek just opening his pack.
He was chubby and plump, a right jolly old elf,
And I lol'd when I saw him in spite of myself.
A wink of his eye and a tweet from his cell,
Soon gave me to know that all was well.
He spoke not a word but went straight to his work,
Checking key pads and iPods, then turned with a jerk.

And laying a finger aside of his nose,
While texting his reindeer, up the chimney he rose.
He sprang to his sleigh, to his team gave a shout,
And away they all flew as my bars all ran out.
Then I watched him text his message to all
Ere his sleigh slowly drove out of sight,
No matter the method, no matter the means,
Merry Christmas to all, and good night.

Clement C. Moore wrote his famous poem "A Visit from St. Nicholas" in 1822. Although Santa is still making his miraculous journey around the globe just as in years gone by, it's possible that today his means of communicating might have changed a bit. I wonder. . . .

Christmas Hotline

At Thanksgiving time it is possible to get food-related questions answered, such as: "How long does it take to thaw a 22-pound turkey?" or "If I stuff the bird, how does that effect the cooking time?" These and many other questions relating to the big feast are answered by "Thanksgiving hotline" services such as those offered on Food Network or by the folks at Butterball. These are great services when answers are desperately needed to make the holiday go smoothly.

Why does it have to be just for Thanksgiving? I have had plenty of questions in the past to keep the elves busy if only there were a Christmas hotline! I could start asking questions the day after Thanksgiving and use such a hot line right up to Christmas day! What I wouldn't give for some advice to help me with my holiday dilemmas!

For instance, over the years we have received beautiful Christmas cards. Aside from a few art projects and package decorating, what can be done with all of them? Oh, for some solution from a Christmas hotline! Then one year I decided to staple the old cards to a long red velvet ribbon and hang it from a fastener high on an entry room wall. Now we have several long ribbons filled with festive cards hanging from many doorways in our home. What I wouldn't have given for a hotline to help me out years ago.

Hotline question #2: What do I do with the tangled mess of tree lights I buy each year when yet another strand of lights goes out? Just getting the lights out of the box and stretching them out to their full length is stressful and difficult. It seems like a strand of 100 lights stretches to all of a foot or two. After many years of unsuccessfully trying to stretch those little midgets to no avail, my husband came up with a solution. He warms the oven to about 200 degrees, turns it off, and then places the tangled mess of lights in the oven for a few minutes. The result? We get a flexible, long strand of tree lights stretching way longer than the original string. Although I'm not really sure that heating tree lights is mentioned in the fine print on the box, it works for us.

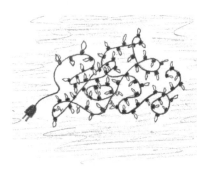

Hotline question #3: When should a family buy their Christmas tree? Will the tree get too dry if bought early? Will the perfect tree still be there if a family waits until later in December to purchase it?

My hotline advice came from a volunteer selling Christmas trees one year. Once the trees are cut, he reminded me, they can wait at the sale lot or in one's own backyard; it's up to the buyer. So now we rise very early the morning after Thanksgiving, borrow an old pick-up truck and drive it out into the country to purchase our perfect tree.

Hotline question #4: "What do I get for my college-age nephew, my book club buddies, the new friend I hardly know, the old friend that I've known for years?" Through trial and error, gift exchanges, return postage, and a few apologies, I wish a hotline service would have shared advice with me long ago in one simple word: consumables! No sizes to worry about, no duplicates, no returns. In my own kitchen I can jams and jellies. I bake holiday breads and cookies. I cook soups, make candy and label homemade salsas to satisfy everyone on my list.

Hotline question #5: When a person can't decorate one more cookie or peel and core one more apple for all those homemade consumable gift ideas, what then? On my list nowadays is a trip to an Illinois winery, a locally owned coffee roaster or a nearby gourmet shop that carries unusual seasonal ideas. Gifts from such places are local and delicious. That's it. Merry Christmas.

Hotline question #6: What if none of these suggestions is appropriate? I have learned through personal experience (thank you very much, Dudley) to buy or make something for a person's pet! It's as appreciated and remembered as any gift one could give to the humans in the family. Ho, ho, woof!

There are so many more questions we could all contribute if only a Christmas hotline existed. I personally have several more questions, except it's time to hang the tree lights, and I think I smell something burning in the oven!

The Spirit of the Season

Spreading the spirit of Christmas is indeed a gift that one can give at this holiday season. Such a gift is neither purchased nor wrapped, but there is no mistaking its presence. Once upon a recent Christmas past I was the recipient of such Christmas spirit.

As the holidays drew near, I was up to my eyeballs in work-related issues and family projects. Nothing was coming together as I had expected, and something had to give! What could I put on hold until next year when things might not be quite so hectic?

What about a smaller Christmas tree? Every year on the day after Thanksgiving we travel outside town to buy our very tall tree. It takes a week or more in early December to place the tree in the stand, string the lights and hang the decorations. Perhaps a smaller tree would work just fine this year. Still, the tree is one aspect of the holiday that involves all our family members, from picking out the perfect pine to hanging the last ornament. Could we skip the big tree this year? No, the tree tradition had to stay.

What about all that holiday baking? Long lines at the store and late hours spent making Christmas goodies can sometimes take the fa-la-la out of the holiday. However, it's that once a year baking of grandma's sugar cookies and my mom's pecan tarts, known to us as tassies, that I enjoy so much, and hopefully others enjoy receiving them. Could I skip the baking this year? The smells of cinnamon and gingerbread wafting from the warm oven as cookies and breads bake is so intertwined with memories of Christmas that I couldn't set it aside. No, the baking had to stay.

Shopping for others is a tradition that certainly has changed over the years for us. Electronic gadgets, big screens and bigger screens have long since replaced toys, guitars, fish tanks and bicycles in this family! Perhaps it was time to cut back on the gift giving. Still, doesn't taking the time and putting forth effort to do something special for someone exemplify a lot of the fun of Christmas? Could we skip all that excitement? No, I couldn't miss out on that wonderful feeling.

And thus as Thanksgiving faded, and Christmas sprinted ever closer like a giant downhill snowball picking up speed, I made my decision. To give myself some wiggle room and to unhustle the bustle of the season, I would not write a holiday essay like I had in years past, and we wouldn't hold the annual

Christmas Eve brunch. There, it was done, and I could now move on to complete other holiday tasks.

That is when this most remarkable spirit of the season came calling. Attending an after-school meeting one day, I ran into Roz, a teaching colleague I hadn't seen for several years. "Every year I look forward to reading your holiday essay," she said. "I can't wait to see what it's going to be about this year." That's all it took. One moment, one example of sharing that Christmas spirit with her kind words, and I knew I would put pen to paper.

Later that week we were having dinner with friends, and I mentioned my plans to cancel the brunch. The couple shared with me that they were delaying their travel plans just so they could attend our Christmas Eve breakfast. Their daughter, who is always invited but kept from attending due to school and work demands, was also looking forward to attending with them this year. And that is all it took, again! The holiday spirit was exemplified by our friends' warm comments as they reminisced about our yearly tradition of sharing food and time together. I knew in a moment the brunch was back on.

The day of the brunch was filled with favorite foods, friends and laughter. Amid all this frivolity and the clearing away of dishes, the doorbell rang. It was Wally, a dear friend and neighbor. He had just stopped by to say how much he had enjoyed my Christmas essay in that morning's *News-Gazette* paper . . . the article I almost didn't write!

And there it was. I had received Christmas gifts that were neither purchased nor wrapped but were given through the kind words of a colleague, through the warm encouragement of friends, and through a heartfelt thank-you that arrived at my door. Such words and wishes given to others are some of the best examples of sharing the true Christmas spirit. And to think, I almost missed it.